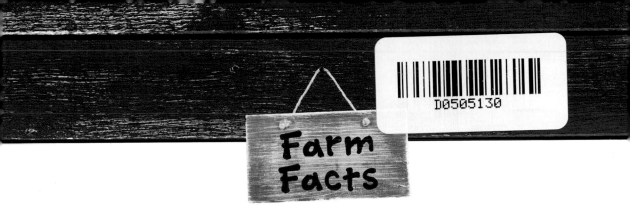

Farm Facts

Buildings on the Farm

by Lisa J. Amstutz

raintree
a Capstone company — publishers for children

Raintree is an imprint of Capstone Global Library Limited, a company incorporated in England and Wales having its registered office at 264 Banbury Road, Oxford, OX2 7DY – Registered company number: 6695582

www.raintree.co.uk
myorders@raintree.co.uk

Edited by Jill Kalz
Picture research by Kelly Garvin
Originated by Capstone Global Library

Designed by Ashlee Suker
Production by Katy LaVigne
Printed and bound in India

ISBN 978 1 4747 6868 9 (hardback)

ISBN 978 1 4747 6884 9 (paperback)

British Library Cataloguing in Publication Data
A full catalogue record for this book is available from the British Library.

Acknowledgements
We would like to thank the following for permission ... photographs: ... shlee Suker, 19; iStockphoto: chuckcollier, backcover, 10 ... 15; Shutterstock: Agatha Koroglu, 20, Arina P Habich, 11, Brenda Carson, 8, Christofotos, 5, inese.online 7, jax10289, 21, Lucian Milasan, 13, Michalakis Ppalis, cover, Mi ... Design Element: Shutterstock: Dudarev Mikhail ... kle ... ...h, Sichon

Every effort has been made to contact copyright holders of material reproduced in this book. Any omissions will be rectified in subsequent printings if notice is given to the publisher.

All the internet addresses (URLs) given in this book were valid at the time of going to press. However, due to the dynamic nature of the internet, some addresses may have changed, or sites may have changed or ceased to exist since publication. While the author and publisher regret any inconvenience this may cause readers, no responsibility for any such changes can be accepted by either the author or the publisher.

Contents

On the farm

Farms have many buildings. There are barns, sheds and stables. There is a farmhouse too! Different buildings do different jobs.

Places for animals

Barns keep farm animals safe and dry. Animals are often kept there at night. Some barns have space outside for the animals too.

Farmers also store straw and hay in barns. Some farm animals, such as cows, eat hay in the winter. Many animals sleep on straw.

straw

hay

Chickens live in a coop. They lay eggs in nest boxes. The coop keeps them safe from foxes.

A stable is a big barn.

Horses sleep in stables.

Each horse has its

own stall.

Other buildings

These tall buildings are silos.
Farmers store grain in them.
The grain can be used to
feed animals in the winter.

Tractors are kept
in a machine shed.
The shed keeps
them dry.

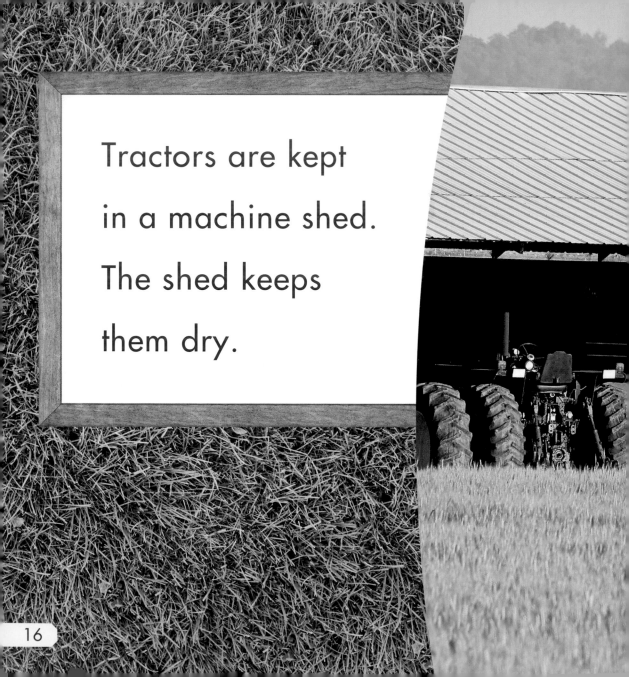

What if a tractor breaks? The farmer might need to fix it. The tools are in the tool shed.

This is a farmhouse.

Who lives here?

The farmer and the

farmer's family!

Glossary

barn a farm building where crops, animals and equipment are kept

grain the seed of a grassy plant, such as wheat, rice, corn, rye or barley

hay dried grasses

machine a piece of equipment that is used to do a job

shed a simple building used for storage

silo a tall, round tower used to store food for farm animals

stable a building where horses are kept

stall the area of a stable where a horse sleeps

straw dried stems of wheat, barley or oat plants

Find out more

Books

A Nature Walk on the Farm (Nature Walks), Louise and Richard Spilsbury (Raintree, 2015)

A Visit to the Farm (Collins Big Cat), Michael Morpurgo (Collins, 2005)

The Farm (A Visit to), Blake Hoena (Raintree, 2019)

Websites

Find out about food and farming in the 5–8 years section: **www.foodafactoflife.org.uk**

Watch a video of a working farm: **www.bbc.com/bitesize/clips/z9qtfg8**

Comprehension questions

1. What are three buildings you may find on a farm?

2. Why are barns useful on a farm?

3. What do you think is the most important farm building? Why?

Index